The Light

A healing poem

Written by:

OFER   COHEN

Translated by: Mali Joy and Arthur Livingstone

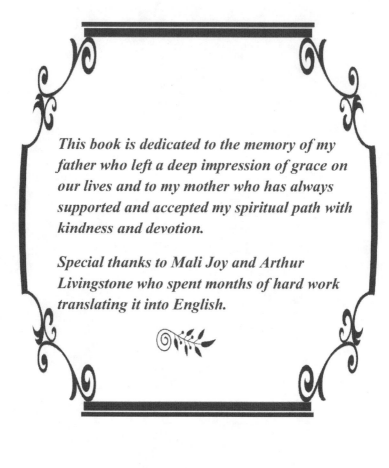

This book is dedicated to the memory of my father who left a deep impression of grace on our lives and to my mother who has always supported and accepted my spiritual path with kindness and devotion.

Special thanks to Mali Joy and Arthur Livingstone who spent months of hard work translating it into English.

Knowing you are light is healing

Experiencing the light is enlightenment

CONTENTS

''experiencing the light is my religion,

it is like a constant reminder of my eternity;

in this beautiful dream call life , I keep being

spontaneous, aware of my true nature ;

I can't remember my first breath but

I do know it's all started much before that;

Naturally without being involve or giving attention,

I allow the light of compassion and love

to penetrate the darkness , a healing light

leading all into a stat of enlightenment.

Ofer

Chapter 1: **The Light**

Light,
The source,
The essence of the cycle.
The temporary is sometimes visible,
The eternal,
Both seeing and not seen,
Carrying spirit or void,
Natural and ever-changing.
Physicality and phenomena,
All manifestations of light.
Thought and spirit,
Are the lights of creation,
Witness to a sense of being.
The eternal is in all things,
It is one light;
The transient is part of its light,
Conscious or insentient,
Appearing and vanishing
Ceaselessly.
The eternal is constant,
Yet difficult to grasp.
To our limited senses it appears to vanish;
In the absence of oblivion,
It is present as existing light.

The Light

One source,
Whose expression is light.
One consciousness,
Filled with light.
A single awareness,
The quintessence
From which souls emanate.
The universal light moves,
Manifesting itself
On different worlds;
The same in essence,
Only in different forms.
A soul is a spark
Of awareness,
Developing gradually,
Beginning in physical worlds,
Evolving slowly to higher worlds,
Until synchronized,
Remerged with the source.

The Light

The cyclical ebb and flow is life,
Its purpose to develop
And integrate with the source.
When the soul enters the body,
The source gives it vitality.
Awake it watches through the third eye;
Sleeping it hovers
Between worlds,
Viewing reality, imagination and dreams,
Moving from past to future.
All that emerges from this is temporary
But results in something essential.
Only the light of the eternal soul,
Is above all this.
Through reincarnations
In the lower worlds,
The soul progresses,
Until coming of age,
It reunites with the source.

The Light

The eternal soul descending like a spirit
Instills life into the body;
From this is separated a ray of light,
The soul that drives
The work of creation,
The essence of pure consciousness.
All memories of the soul's reincarnations are
Hidden deep in the subconscious
To ensure concentration
On the task.
From the day of its birth,
The soul flows like water,
With few moments of stillness,
Absorbing deep memories,
Dissolving with love and suffering,
Mingled with mere moments of happiness,
Contemplating at the end of life,
Returning to embrace the source.

The Light

Little by little
Consciousness forms,
Clear and cloudy, strong or weak,
In control or out of control,
Intent on finding itself;
Wandering from joy to sadness,
Sometimes suffering,
That is the way to grow,
Roaming without motive,
Fulfilling another stage
In the cycle of evolution.
Like a morning's droplet of dew
That evaporates into an ocean of light,
To be gathered back into the sea.

The Light

One's soul is a light vibrating,
From physicality with its spark of spirit
To a transparent soul,
Illuminated and tranquil.
Physicality and survival are evolution,
From an individual awareness in search of meaning
To an enlightened consciousness
That is part of the overall light.
One is surrounded by light
Perpetually flowing and creating.
Release of the eternal soul from the cycles of evolution,
Depends on the development,
Of a soul aware of itself.
It needs not seclusion or retreat,
But silent observation with altruistic love,
And the development of compassion
For every living and inanimate thing;
This is the purification of the soul
And its return to the light.
When the consciousness is aware and lucid,
The eternal soul spreads light and love.
When the body disappears, only flowing light remains
And the need to reincarnate ceases.
Thus in the void
You are part of the source;
Only then is the cycle complete.

The Light

Soul and body,
Are surrounded by light.
Mountains, sea, sun and moon,
Are all manifestations of light;
Light penetrating from above
And returning back.
As substance it motivates the cycle,
Intangible it is everything.
The light flickers and is difficult to retrieve;
Distraction and knowledge obscure it.
Through the physical it gives vitality,
Through the spirit it bestows eternity.
Sadness and suffering are light that is absent,
Happiness and love are light in abundance.
Merger with the light Is spiritual elevation,
Emptiness is loss of light;
Thoughtful observation replenishes,
Awakening on the path to illumination,
And when the light is revealed
In the consciousness,
The body abounds with serene energy,
Emptiness swelling with happiness,
Without motive and without purpose .

The Light

All occurs in a cycle.
Awareness of the cycle
Is paramount.
Everything moves incessantly
In the cosmic cycle;
Earth, wind, sea and fire,
Energy changing form,
Visible and invisible.
In one's cycle
Light flows in constant renewal,
Cells are created and die,
All in known and organized codes.
The life of one cell
Is as the life
Of an entire being.
One's light is part of the light
Of an entire universe,
All reliant on
And nourished by each other.
Ignorance is partial sight,
Deep feeling is deceptive,
Suffering comes from disconnection,
Happiness from unity,
Unity with the source.

The Light

Birth and death are like
Body and consciousness.
One's heart is flowing fire;
The heart of the universe
Is boiling magma,
All are manifestations
Of the light of life,
A cycle of cause and result,
But its source is in one light.
One is charged with life's spirit
Or depleted,
Finally crumbling to lifeless dust.
The purpose of the change
Is release.
Air and fire impel the senses,
Water and earth stimulate intention,
The spirit's wanderings spur will.
As the water is deep,
So is the feeling,
As the fire is intense,
So is passion and love.
Thinking precedes action;
Only the spark of the eternal soul,
Is beyond all conception
Or anything that has form.

The Light

The light source
Is seen and unseen,
It flows and changes shape incessantly.
Suns and stars, hot and cold,
Continents and oceans,
Fauna and flora,
All is flowing light.
A spark of the soul naturally pulses,
Every living thing
Is like a radiant star;
The light of the universe
Penetrates the eyes,
Driving the consciousness
And breathing,
Nourishing a creature's thoughts,
Keeping the secret of evolution.
When its flow becomes weaker
In a living being, it loses vitality,
Like a flame that has lost its strength,
Bestowed its light
And consumed its substance by burning,
So the light of the soul
Returns to the source,
Until it re-manifests
In the light of another body.

Part II: **Man's Light**

One's light is as the source,
From a tiny spark to a flowing beam,
Will and desire are created of the flow,
The elements fan the flame.
Air and fire are a spark of the light,
Water and substance are creation;
That's the essence of the mystery.
Beginning with a spark and a tender spirit
To a complete body, earth and sea,
Light is in unceasing motion.
In hidden worlds the dimension of time is absent
But here light is measured in time;
Although as it evolves it changes shape,
Or expresses itself variously,
Its character remains eternal and fixed.

Man's Light

One's light,
A point of light, a spark of awareness;
Human light is charged with life and thought;
A soul will accumulate memories and strife;
A spirit is on a quest.
Breath and senses are proof of our existence.
An identity that will change
With the years,
Mostly concerned with ephemeral objects,
Yearns for a love that blurs the senses.
With breath emotions arise,
Pleasure and pain merge alternately
As if to demonstrate the lust for life.

Man's Light

One's light has centers
For absorbing,
Allowing the light of the universe
To flow and nourish the aura.
Light from above flows into the eyes
And out again in circles of spirit
Around the body.
The eternal light surrounds the visible light,
And when the soul is charged
With the good energy
The break in the continuum
Of the flow is made whole.
The body's light, inhaling and exhaling
Are the motions of consciousness;
Thought and emotion are
The light's vibration;
Spirit and body are interdependent,
Constantly affected by density
And the way the light is scattered.

Man's Light

Man creates his world
With pure intentness.

> The light of thought
> Creates reality every minute,
> Changes and creates
> Shape and phenomena.

From place to place
From hour to hour,
Man is a victim of
Cause and result.

> If not hoarded,
> The light dissipates,
> The body is drained,
> And the spirit knows no rest.

When the ability to absorb
Is damaged and the flow interrupted,
Apathy or illness are
The only result.

> It appears as old age;
> With death the light flows on
> To a new birth.

Man's Light

Memory and thought
Pursue and are pursued.
As drops in the ocean
Change into a cloud,
Thought are but echoes of memories,
Sea and cloud are light
In a visible cycle;
Memories and thoughts
Are in a hidden cycle.
You can change a river's course,
But it will always reach the sea,
And as sea and rain merge into one,
Thoughts become memories,
Forgotten flashes of the light's oscillations.
And everything done
Was created by the light of thought,
Vibrations of the energy of creation.
And everything is created by thought,
Is destined to merge
With the source,
Like an echo that returns and vanishes
And a dream forgotten on the morrow.

Man's Light

Humanity's destiny,
Cycles without beginning or end;
Consciousness wanders
In the circle of evolution,
Life in changing light.
With death light departs.
What is revealed is not the root,
But only the edge of the cycle.
The physical alters endlessly
And the light of the universe
Is in constant movement.
One is in thrall to the
Enchantment of evolution,
Incessantly pondering.
Life and death seem opposites
But they are just two points,
In the circle of the light of creation.
And in a moment of clarity a thought appears
Bringing enlightenment.
The choice is yours;
If you let go,
The light of awareness will be revealed,
There is an understanding
That nothing can be grasped;
If oblivion returns
You remain in the same place.

Man's Light

Awareness of the light's existence
Increases naturalness
And encourages internal conquest.
Thought and emotion deepen commitment
And encourage conquest of the external.
Inner achievement involves
Hoarding and preserving the light,
External achievements are empty entities.
Empty strives to be full
And full aspires to be emptied.
Words and deeds are short-lived,
Because life changes their meaning.
Adherence to the nature of things
Is wise and simple;
Ignoring this deepens ignorance.
Conquering the physical is success,
Renouncing it is enlightenment.
Exposing the light
Is adhering to the natural.
Acknowledging this will lead to enlightenment.
Sorrow and suffering are rooted in illusion,
As all phenomena revert to quiescence
And what was will be again;
Understanding the contradiction,
Is the beginning of enlightenment.

Man's Light

Compared to the life of the universe,
One's light is short-lived
And the life of a mosquito is negligible;
But the light is not lost,
It only transforms.
There is an unknown number
Of dimensions in the cycle,
In which the light of awareness is expressed in different ways;
But they are all manifestations
Of the source light cycle.
The light of the body, soul and thought are
Expressions of one's light
And a way to develop the eternal soul
By aspiring to be free
And merge with the source.
It is important to remember and internalize this
So as to avoid making distinctions
And having a mistaken perception.
When the light of awareness becomes thought
It begets a new reality,
But that is only part of the development
Of the eternal soul.
The extra-sensory is hard to prove
But exposing the light is the correct way
To understand the purpose of evolution.

Man's Light

One's light changes shape
In the cycle,
Its flow in the body is slow and compressed;
In the eternal soul it is nimble.
At the end the light is gathered in
And united with the source.
The process of change holds an important secret;
Life begins with inhalation
And Death with expiration,
But in the cycle of the light this is just
A change of density,
Like breathing in and breathing out,
The starting point is illusion
And time cannot be measured,
There is no beginning or end;
The transformations
Are an ever-changing phenomenon.

Man's Light

Earth's light and starlight
Incessantly flow and merge,
As do the light of awareness and one's light.
The awareness is the breathing in,
Endlessly charging with light;
That is the eternal cycle.
Only its density and its state
Testify to the power of illusion.
But here knowledge is enough;
Rising above ignorance.
Don't cling to distinctions,
Because what began with birth,
Ends with being gathered into silence.
Physicality and its purpose are not an end in themselves,
But only stations of light to serve the eternal soul;
And the end of the entire cycle is pure,
The unification of the eternal soul's light,
Its nature being to unite with the source.

Man's Light

One's light is as the light of the universe,
Flowing and merging,
Appearing as the essence of evolution.
Sea, earth, wind, fire and awareness,
Are an active essence of latent light.
The merger of the elements causes spontaneous creation.
Everything around is evidence;
Spontaneous creation and tranquility,
Flowing light, basic to its nature.
Only those who are aware of their temporality,
Who see every animate and inanimate thing as part of their light
And avoid making absolute distinctions,
See the world in themselves.
With love of all the hold on the physical disappears,
And the tranquility of the source is gradually revealed.
Thoughts and events continue to pass by
And one remains at the center of evolution,
Radiating love like a shimmering light.
The past disappears and only the present exists,
Remains as a witness to one's existence until death,
When the light of one's eternal soul
Merges once more with the source.

Man's Light

The soul develops in the body
As a spark of consciousness,
Distinguishing and seeing.
As it gains strength the light of awareness is hidden,
Through feelings and attention the soul creates everything around.
It is a void that fills with content,
Shapes and phenomena create identity,
Thoughts and actions shape personality,
The essence of consciousness becomes a mirror.
One's light seeps out
As the soul absorbs and experiences
The cycle of life and death.
When it turns its gaze on life,
Its attention is distracted from the eternal soul
And it forgets.

Man's Light

Between moments of happiness and grief,
The purpose of evolution develops
And comes to fulfillment.
And the nature of the soul changes with time
And learns to preserve its light
As it merges with the light of consciousness.
Then one's light illuminates the shadows
And everything is discovered to be wraithlike.
When the content of the illusion disappears,
Serenity is discovered,
Enlightenment arising from profound understanding
Is the way back to the spark of the eternal soul.

Man's Light

Consciousness is water,
The source of life.
Energy is the fire of love.

Spirit drives intention,
Carnality is of the earth.

Water and fire create thinking,
Spirit and substance energize action
That's the secret of the cycle of evolution.
And the result can be sensed.

As evidence of which,

Like a restless engine,
You are trapped in dreams of doing,
When this is understood the miracle happens.
As with love that has passed, you are left wondering
Not understanding who the dreamer that dreamt is
And in fact you never existed.

Man's Light

Deep in the illusion,
Pleasure, suffering and pain,
You are like a shadow among ghosts,
A spirit amidst shadows,
Deep within, if you purify your soul
And recognize your light
And not what you thought you were,
Then the good energy changes,
You light up the shadows,
Illuminating the correct path for all;
Internal happiness develops spontaneously,
And your light is illumination.

Man's Light

Man's soul, like a flickering light,
Wandering from dimension to dimension,
Renouncing pure light for the illusion of acquisition.
Ignorance and oblivion are the source of suffering and pain.
The remedy has long been with you,
Awareness of the cycle is the cure,
Just knowing this heals,
Then the light flows clearly,
Without pause or disconnect.
Only when the soul is purified,
Does the light of awareness become visible.
It is important to understand:
The source of suffering is in the seeking,
The source of pain is in resistance,
The source of happiness is in letting go,
The nature of happiness is acceptance,
Life is composed of opposition and unity,
Then creation and change are received with love,
Criticality and separation will distance love,
Deep awareness is a movement within yourself.

Man's Light

Creation and change are like birth and death;
They are vibrations of the light of thought,
Courage is an opportunity for liberation.
When the soul is wandering
All is disunity;
Everything is to be judged,
That is the reason for our limitations.
The concept of self belongs to the temporary.
If the nature of the temporary is change of form
Then there is no loss,
Basically this is the light of awareness.
Here only seeing the phenomena is revealing the light
In preparation for merging.
The eternal resides between the thoughts;
The eternal is indefinable,
But it is the natural foundation.
You might say it always exists
But is hidden most of the time,
And when you adhere to the natural,
You move towards the source.

Man's Light

Need and security are the basis of faith,
And many believe they know best,
But any claim of uniqueness is misleading,
Because everything is one,
And the one is in everything.
Beyond every distinction
There is basically one light
And it has many names,
But it is one and uniform.
Remember your own light
And you are at one with the natural;
Remove yourself from all distinction and avoid division,
Nature is already as complete as you are perfect.
Nature is the merging of tranquility with what exists.
Natural is light, light in a cycle,
Like a river flowing unobstructed to the sea.
Resistance comes from thoughts,
Fluctuation is different from flowing;
Acceptance is wisdom;
Better to teach adaptation than to develop resistance.
When you merge you become one;
When you divide you split apart,
That's the difference between the darkness of oblivion
And merging with the source.

Man's Light

All rivers flow to the sea
But the sea is not full;
All the doctrines speak of the same one
And promise a result,
And what is difficult to prove,
Already exists within you.
Many words lose their meaning;
Everything can be described by tranquility.
In the visible world everything is a phenomenon
And every end is a new beginning,
Everything exists but is waiting to be discovered.
If you abandon the idea of making distinctions
Your reality will become one of love.
If you expect too much
You will experience great disappointment.
The universal light is all around you,
One's light aspires to unite,
Like male and female,
Yet both are from the same source.
It requires naturalness to see the light,
When the light is absent there is only forgetfulness.
Living in the light inspires unity,
An identity that dissolves into the source.

Man's Light

There are many ways and many disciples,
Great teachers have their methods,
But the light has ever-changing dimensions,
So their claim to being unique is misleading.
One is part of the whole
And the whole is gathered into the one.
What is ever-changing creates controversy,
Because the cycle is expressed in many ways.
However, there is no need to strain
To understand the purpose.
Partial insight requires effort,
Remove the effort and the way is shortened.
Abandon all notions
With the understanding that there is no fragmentation
Then gaze at the change with wonder
And avoid making definitions.
Because everything in the cycle is in constant motion,
Temporary, albeit with purpose and cause,
To know the way is the goal.
Physical light is the beginning,
You are a witness to your being in a state of tranquility,
Being within an emptiness of love,
That is your natural state, it is not a doctrine,
This is the secret of enlightenment.

Man's Light

The answer lies within,
To claim uniqueness is to show
A lack of understanding.
One has the power
To enlighten a nation
But also to mislead an entire world.
Many words have the power to deceive,
But the worst is to deceive oneself.
Foolishly everyone thinks that they
Have sole right to the truth,
But all the doctrines are mere passing thoughts.
Nature was born without sin,
And the source of many is one,
Thus all creatures are equal sons of light.
It is our individual destiny to return to the source,
What is apparent is fated to change.
History, too, repeats itself
Eluding permanency,
The application of force accelerates external change,
Internal change requires tranquility.
The transient world is driven by control and power,
The eternal world by tranquility and love.

Chapter 3: **The Light of Awareness**

One's consciousness is breathing,
Universal consciousness is light concealed,
Its nature like a flickering flame,
Clear and pure at source,
Partly concealed and hard to grasp,
Partly clinging to the soul's light,
Allowing it to be seen.
During the day it watches and observes,
At night as it floats in higher worlds,
It dreams of release from the burden of life,
Returning each morning
To participate in life's journey.
Life and death, youth and old age,
A world of sounds and quivering thought,
Thus the cycle of the light of evolution is sustained.

The Light of Awareness

The light's cycle is the purpose;
In the physical world this can be seen all around.
From consciousness to thought, from soul to awareness,
All this is the light's creation.
The soul is an expression of the spirit,
Consciousness is an expression of existence.
The light of thought is
The heartbeat of awareness;
It flows with the breath.
In the universe it is the source that creates all,
In the individual it is the light of thought,
But what is sensed and seen
Is the light of consciousness,
When the soul is distracted by activity,
Its fate endlessly changes,
Life is cause and result,
But when it is aroused from the illusion of activity,
The mind is cleared and the light of awareness is exposed.
Through tranquility one merges with the cycle of evolution.

The Light of Awareness

Above in the heavens
Is blue light with occasional clouds.
Below in nature
The roots of a tree are not seen;
Clouds nourish the roots,
Man destiny is a result of his thoughts,
Part of the cycle of light.
When the clouds disappear the sky is clear,
Clarity of thought is enlightenment.
There is nothing to grasp and
Nothing to hold on to,
Between the thoughts lies peace of mind.

The Light of Awareness

Thought is like clouds passing across the sky,
The light of a thought is like the vapor of the clouds.
Formations change,
Rapidly evolving,
Sometimes flickering,
And with every inhalation a thought arises
Creating a new reality,
And with every exhalation,
One's light is in a changing reality.
But the knowledge that oblivion exists,
Is also the way to liberation;
When the soul releases its hold,
One ceases to identify with objects
And the light is revealed in its simplicity.
This is the beginning of merging
When the light of consciousness unites once again with the source.

The Light of Awareness

And when the soul lets go of all thought of activity,

Awakens from the illusion,

And loses the need to have form,

Then the nature of creation changes;

Man becomes pure light,

Serene light penetrates the clouds

And that is enlightenment.

The Light of Awareness

At birth
One's soul separates from the eternal soul,
The light of consciousness takes form.
If the light is concealed,
And the soul distracted from seeing the source,
The choice is lost.
There is only
Sensory awareness,
Cause and result,
Groping in the dark.
Life and death are a return to the wanderings of the eternal soul.
Better to choose the easy way,
Observing life without making distinctions.
Each time the light of awareness becomes thought,
There is a process of creation,
Herein is the secret of enlightenment.
Recollection and evolution occur spontaneously;
Forgetfulness and activity lead to expectation.
That is the difference between accumulating the light
And allowing it to seep away.

The Light of Awareness

When the light is concealed,
The soul is mesmerized by thought,
Losing itself in a quest after purpose.
All is distraction,
Identification and forgetfulness.
Life moves from building to destroying,
Events leave a deep impression,
Memories of what was.
When the soul is exhausted from holding on,
At breaking point,
The light of awareness is revealed for an instant,
Filling with the rare content of enlightenment.
The soul experiences tranquility for the first time
And the world around is a reflection of reality.
The light of the good energy is revealed,
New insight is emerges,
And it is simple to understand
The depth of ignorance.

The Light of Awareness

The light of awareness flows with the breath,
Constantly becoming thoughts.
Thoughts and senses
Deepen the experience of life,
Create feelings and strong desires,
And with such constant attention,
Create every phenomenon.
Awakening begins with the light
Of the breath;
It is meditation on the light of awareness.
Knowledge is all you need
To break the dependence on thought.
You have to look at thought
And purify its content,
Without judgment or desire for any return.
If you are not engaged in activity
You are already protected from making distinctions.
Thoughts and more thoughts pass by
And you are in the center of the light of awareness.
The spark of emancipation already exists;
The light of the soul naturally merges
 With the source.

The Light of Awareness

Lack of involvement
Does not hinder development,
It is only an enlightened approach
To the reality of the light.
Little by little,
The illusion of your existence dissolves.
Thus the light of the soul merges
With the source,
United with the infiniteness
Of the light of the cycle.
This is eternality.
The sensation from the light is love,
Its nature to unite,
Desire and forgetting naturally delay the process.
The love of the light is clear awareness;
It is like non-existence
In what appears to be existence.
Regaining the memory
Is the secret of the way back.

The Light of Awareness

The universe and life are in constant movement,
Energy drives and consciousness creates,
Only the vibrations change.
Awareness of the light releases us from dependency;
The light of the soul
Relaxes its grip
And is released from the bonds of evolution.
The light of awareness induces peace of mind,
One's light illuminates the darkness for all;
It is the soul's awakening
In which consciousness changes,
The direction of the flow changes,
The source light is gathered in
And flows back up in a cycle.
The seepage of light ceases,
It is the purification of the consciousness,
A sincere testimony to enlightenment,
A smile for no reason,
The selfless love of all,
A complete antidote to avarice.

The Light of Awareness

Emotions, sadness and joy,
Are the wanderings of the soul's light in consciousness.
Dreams are a gentle fluttering
Of the light of consciousness
In its nightly manifestation as thought.
Life is continuous evolution,
Waves in the cycle of light.
What is built is destined to disappear
And acquisitions are destined to pall.
Love of one is human,
Love of many is eternal,
Strong passions are an overflow of the light
But with lack of it will fade away
As fire is extinguished by rain and frost.
Memories pile up layer upon layer
And yet you seek the light.
War and peace serve the ignorant,
People and events are but the vibrations of life,
And who will remember previous generations.

The Light of Awareness

When a baby take its first breath,
That is the moment of birth
When the light of the eternal soul is revealed for an instant.
Then the individual soul splits from the eternal
Creating its own entity,
A vibration of the light of consciousness.
And with each moment that the light of awareness
Becomes thought, it deepens.
This is the seeing soul seeking meaning for itself,
And every breath brings an experience,
Waves of emotion and sensation deepen its existence.
The nature of the physical
Is to intensify the memory loss;
Man becomes a kind of machine,
Trapped in a bubble of
Cause and result.

The Light of Awareness

A sequence of thoughts has the power to shape reality;
Through attention we create perception.
If the source of attention is
The light of awareness that has become thought,
Then the senses are the creator of perception,
Turning the light of thought into evolution;
And like a name given at birth
The light of thought creates form.
It takes profound understanding
To see the illusion.
The lights seeps away when the soul is distracted,
Creating ephemeral objects.
Knowing this process is only the beginning,
Meditating on it is the solution.
Thus the nature of man returns to the source
Where lies the secret of enlightenment,
Which is only to observe
Without identifying and without
Being involved in the result;
This is the remedy.

The Light of Awareness

The stages of the cycle must be committed to memory:
First the light of consciousness creates thought,
Thoughts are consciousness in action.
This is where the split begins.
Light flowing into the senses
Creates perception,
An overflow of light creates a multitude of thoughts.
This is the source of preoccupation.
Preoccupation is the source of the seepage,
Hiding the light of awareness,
And when the light flows from inside to out
The soul is trapped in a temporary dimension;
Impressions arise and create experience
And one lives in a bubble of one's creation.
Thus the connection with the source is lost;
This is forgetfulness.
The remerging of one's light with the source
Is the purpose of emancipation.
It is easy to achieve;
At first only knowledge is required;
Profound understanding slowly evolves;
This is the beginning of enlightenment.

The Light of Awareness

Believe you are perfect;
It is the beginning of the way back to innocence.
Suddenly the difficult way is repugnant
And what is unnatural is like a sickness,
Drawing trouble to you,
And you have long had what is natural;
Because originally you are pure light.
By seeing the problem
You can love yourself once again,
Love of self is love of the world,
Because the one you includes everything
And the light around includes you.
This is the understanding that leads to enlightenment.

The Light of Awareness

Unconditionally and with no fixation on a goal
You loosen the bonds,
Perceive what never perishes,
Give up ideas about acquiring objects,
Because nature has no need of improvement.
Then the light of awareness is revealed to you.
In life it will be considered capitulation
But in eternity it is the conquest of the illusion.
That is the easy way,
The right way;
You need not strain to attain it
For it is already there within.
The entire secret is in having
The courage to return to innocence.
Knowledge of the light
Fires imagination and creativity,
And there are no more questions.
In nature it is a return to light of awareness,
Merging with the source.

The Light of Awareness

Man's light is as the source light
And no distinction should be made.
The changes in density are the root of the illusion.
The light of the soul is a manifestation of awareness
Keeping life conscious,
And part of it is hidden away in the subconscious.
Convinced of the existence of shadows.
Consciousness shapes our awareness of life.
But that's the nature of the light of awareness
On its way to purifying the soul;
From the pure moment of birth,
The happiness and suffering it experiences
Is its purification by the light
In preparation for merging with the source.

The Light of Awareness

The limits of the light of awareness
When it becomes part of the soul
Can be observed
In inhalation and exhalation,
In the thinking process,
In youth and old age.
The soul has a mechanism for adaptation and defense
That prevents it from having to confront its past
When it is conscious.
Concealing the original source of its light
It is also an obstacle to its release.
When it is in the body it stubbornly
Searches for a purpose,
Like a stream carving through a rock
Searching for an outlet.
At night it wanders
Distancing itself in dreams;
Past, present, future
Lose meaning.
But all this has a purpose and a reason;
Through happiness and suffering
The soul is reunited with the source.

The Light of Awareness

Like fire in contact with water,
At the moment of birth
When the first breath is taken,
The spirit enters
And activates the body like a machine.
The connection is a new one… pure at first,
Instinctively evolving.
At first it is simple,
The light of the soul is wholly natural
And when the elements combine, physical being is created,
And behind it all the light of awareness.
As it is in the nature of light to merge,
The soul absorbs sensory experience,
Parents' love and practicing customs
Names and events, objects and colors.
The secret of enlightenment is to be aware of the light;
Through awareness we dispel the darkness;
It is simply a childhood memory.
Leaving no need for explanations
You flow naturally with the light.

Part 4: **Understanding**

One's will, society and location
Are the main causes of forgetfulness,
Distracting the soul
From remembering the source.
But know that even when
There is seepage of the light
And its vibrations are constantly changing,
There are still many moments of recall.
If emotions are the limitation,
Then observing them will restore the memory.
Even when the light is hidden,
There is a flicker of recall,
Because what is natural lasts forever.
Effortlessly
The light refills.
Changing ones approach builds confidence.
Pure attention focuses on the right objective,
And once more memories of the source are retrieved.

Understanding

Everything in the universe moves in a cycle.
All light returns to itself.
If day is light filling,
Night is light emptying
And so forth.
Life and death are mere events,
Changes in the appearance and density
Of the light of awareness.
Like a dreamer unaware of his dreaming
The soul is trapped in struggles for survival.
Happiness and pain are patterns of the flow,
Oscillations in the cycle of seepage.
And seeing the shadows
The illusion is born,
Opinions and beliefs arise
Of existence and what is beyond existence,
But basically it is one light.
When there is enlightenment
One is like the first ray of light,
Filling the darkness,
Moving from ignorance to merging with the light.

Understanding

You have to recognize you have a choice
And do not allow yourself to be coerced.
Even if you have no choice,
The mere knowledge is enough
To break the pattern that causes forgetfulness.
Let the shadows go for a moment
And you will feel immediate relief;
But remember,
You can only slow the light of thought,
Fools they are who claim they can stop it.
Merge with the light from knowledge
And do not block it.
The renunciation will be achieved without effort.
A truth that is easy to comprehend
Is that the concept of ownership is rotten at the core;
All is transient and cannot be possessed.
Remembering the light within
Is the beginning of your healing
From the sickness of the pursuit.

Understanding

It is indeed sometimes hard to begin
From the point of oblivion,
But like a drowning man with nothing to hang onto,
There is in loss and despair
A spark of enlightenment.
And there is no difference between pleasure, happiness and pain,
These are only turning points
In the vibration of the light's flow.
Exit from ignorance
Is through knowing that the bubble of illusion must be burst,
Then life takes on a different meaning,
The light around you
Reflects the light of awareness,
A sign of merging.
You can feel the change immediately,
Both in the eternal soul and in the thinking process.
The fear of the unknown disappears,
Life and death are like one light,
Wakefulness and forgetfulness,
Sleeping and waking,
From unaware consciousness to enlightenment,
The source light is once again you.

Understanding

Remember:
Only the knowledge that you are
Part of the source light is important.
Light is expressed in the soul through the senses
In the cycle of reproduction.
But when the merging is enabled
One's light reunites with the source.
Enlightenment is here and now,
Without effort or will.
The first spark of remembrance
Is suddenly kindled.
Its light is always there
And only needs to be revealed.
Knowing that it is there
Allows the reunification now.
It's a good beginning.
When you start to feel the tranquility,
The light of awareness swells,
The seepage is stopped,
The flow changes direction,
There is a sense of oneness,
And you become a mirror reflecting the source light.

Understanding

It is important only to know
That the light merges naturally.
Any manipulation of thought
Will be interpreted as interference;
Then the direction of evolution changes.
Shun narrow definitions or judgments,
There is no need for fanaticism, retreat or extreme discipline.
From the moment the idea of self is let go,
The illusion melts away,
Then nothing interferes with the flow.
This is an insight that expands the tranquility.
There is order in nature and also in the cycle of light.
Simple seeing
Produces pure involvement.
With no burden you feel light,
Words lose their meaning,
Your existence is an inspiration
That draws dormant sons of light towards you,
This is perpetual flowing
With the source light.

Understanding

Man creates his world
With pure intentness.

> The light of thought
> Creates reality every minute.
> Changes and creates
> Shape and phenomena.

From place to place,
From hour to hour,
Man is a victim of
Cause and result.

> If not hoarded
> The light dissipates
> The body is drained
> And the spirit knows no rest

When the ability to absorb the light
And the flow is disturbed,
Apathy or illness is the only result,
It appears as old age;
With death as a preparation for rebirth.

Made in the USA
Charleston, SC
31 January 2013